Citizenship

by Anne Miranda
illustrated by Allan M. Burch

Harcourt

Orlando   Boston   Dallas   Chicago   San Diego

Visit *The Learning Site!*

www.harcourtschool.com

Hi! I am Anne American, girl historian. I'm here to talk to you about citizenship and the Constitution of the United States.

What does citizenship mean to you? You probably haven't had to think about being a citizen very much. Our citizenship and our rights are guaranteed by the Constitution, but most of us take them for granted. We are simply used to the freedoms we have.

We feel free to express our opinions. We allow others to express theirs. We read newspapers or watch TV to find out what is going on in the world. We worship or not, as we please. We gather together for discussions. We vote to elect people to positions in the government. These are some of the rights we all have as citizens of the United States.

If you were born in any of the fifty states, you automatically became a citizen of the United States. This right is granted to you by the Fourteenth Amendment of the Constitution, by the way. We'll talk about that later.

Still, how does someone who was not born in the United States become a citizen? The process is called "naturalization." It takes several years to become a naturalized citizen and involves several steps and requirements.

Becoming a citizen is a long and sometimes difficult process. However, the benefits of citizenship make it all worthwhile.

For a person who was not born in the United States, these steps are necessary to become a citizen:

1. Move to the United States.
2. Become a legal resident of the United States. This means applying for and receiving a green card. A green card shows that the person is living legally in this country.
3. Live in the United States for five consecutive years before applying for citizenship. For example, a person who came to the United States in May 1995 could apply for citizenship in May 2000.
4. Apply, or petition, to become a citizen.

Petitioners, the people asking for citizenship, must pass several tests before citizenship can be granted and a certificate of citizenship can be issued. Each petitioner must come before an examiner, who will test the petitioner's readiness. Then the petitioner is obliged to:

1. Prove that he or she can read, write, and speak English.
2. Show that he or she is of good moral character.
3. Show that he or she believes in the principles of the Constitution.
4. Demonstrate an understanding of the government and history of the United States.
5. Take an oath of allegiance to the United States.

Fortunately, children do not have to go through this process. Only people eighteen years old or older have to become naturalized. When parents become naturalized citizens, their children also become citizens of the United States.

Once a person is a citizen, that person gains the rights and freedoms granted under the Constitution of the United States. That person's children gain these rights as well.

But what is the Constitution? What rights does it grant us?

The Constitution of the United States is a document that was created in 1787, after we gained our independence from Great Britain. It was written during the Constitutional Convention, a meeting held in Philadelphia. Many great leaders, including George Washington and Benjamin Franklin, attended the Constitutional Convention.

These patriots, called the Founders, decided what kind of government we would have and how that government should work. They formed three branches of government: the legislative branch to make laws, the executive branch to carry out the laws, and the judicial branch to decide the meaning of laws.

At the time the Constitution was written, it contained bold ideas that have resounded ever since. In adopting the Constitution, we changed from a country where the King had all the rights and power into a country where the people had the rights and power.

Within this amazing document, the Founders identified rights they thought each citizen of the United States should have. These rights are listed in the Constitution as amendments. The first ten amendments of the Constitution are called the Bill of Rights.

Let me briefly explain the Bill of Rights. I should also make sure I've apologized. To whom? To the Founders, for changing the wording just a bit.

Bill of Rights

1. The people have freedom of religion, freedom of speech, freedom of the press, freedom to meet together, and the right to petition the government.

2. People have the right to carry arms (weapons).

3. People do not have to house soldiers during peacetime.

4. People are not subject to unreasonable search and seizure of their persons or property.

5. A person accused of a crime has the right to a trial by jury. A person does not have to give evidence against himself or herself. A person's life, liberty, or property cannot be taken unfairly.

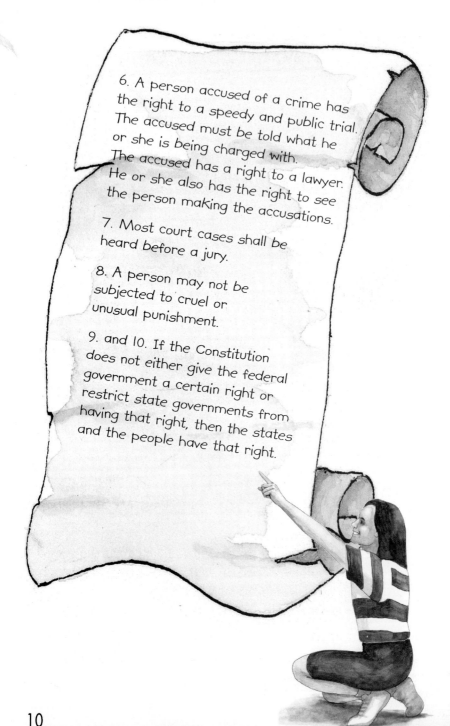

6. A person accused of a crime has the right to a speedy and public trial. The accused must be told what he or she is being charged with. The accused has a right to a lawyer. He or she also has the right to see the person making the accusations.

7. Most court cases shall be heard before a jury.

8. A person may not be subjected to cruel or unusual punishment.

9. and 10. If the Constitution does not either give the federal government a certain right or restrict state governments from having that right, then the states and the people have that right.

Do I hear a cheer from your classroom? The people who framed our Constitution did a brilliant job of planning it, didn't they? The government they designed has lasted for more than two hundred years. It has survived war and peace. It has survived times of prosperity and depression.

The Founders even thought of a plan for adding new amendments to our Constitution. There are now twenty-seven amendments in all. It would be a good exercise in citizenship to read the entire Constitution to find out about your government and to see what all of your rights really are.

Millions of people have come from around the globe to become United States citizens. They came and continue to come to seek the freedoms our Constitution grants them. In return, these people enrich our country. They bring their languages, food, customs, dreams, and ideas.

The United States of America has a culture that combines the cultures of the rest of the world. That is why it is often called the "melting pot." Look around you. See how many signs of different cultures you can find. The United States would be a different place without the influence of so many cultures.

If you had to take a citizenship test, do you think you would know enough about your own country to pass? Let's see.

I am going to ask you questions that an examiner might ask someone who is seeking citizenship. Let's begin with some easy ones!

1. What are the colors of our flag?

2. How many states are there in the United States?

3. What is the White House?

4. What day of the year is Independence Day?

5. Who was the first President of the United States?

ANSWERS: 1. red, white, and blue; 2. fifty; 3. the residence of the President of the United States; 4. the Fourth of July; 5. George Washington

These questions are a little more difficult. Reread the text to find the answers if you get stumped.

6. What is the Constitution?

7. What do we call a change to the Constitution?

8. How many of these changes have been added to the Constitution?

9. What are the three branches of our government?

10. In what year was the Constitution written?

ANSWERS: 6. document that establishes our form of government and grants certain rights to the people of the United States; 7. an amendment; 8. twenty-seven; 9. legislative, executive, and judicial; 10. 1787

Here are some really hard questions. You may have to look up the answers in a history book.

If you already know the answers to these questions, that's SUPER!

11. What is Congress?

12. How many senators are there in Congress?

13. What is the judicial branch of our government?

14. Who heads the executive branch of the government?

15. What special group advises the President?

That last question was really
hard! I hope I have helped you learn
about the Constitution and the
importance of being a citizen.

When you get home, ask a family
member to explain how you came to
be a citizen of the United States.
Were you born here? Were you
naturalized? Were your ancestors
born here? How did they arrive?
Where did they come from?
If anyone at home knows the story, it
is bound to be interesting. You might
find out many things you did not
know before.

This is Anne American,
girl historian, saying good-bye
and good luck.